FOX TALBOT
Photographer

FOX TALBOT
Photographer

———

ROBERT LASSAM

Foreword by Sir Cecil Beaton

COMPTON PRESS
in association with Dovecote Press

To Margaret, my wife
and to the memory of Miss Matilda Talbot CBE
granddaughter of William Henry Fox Talbot

© Robert Lassam 1979

First jointly published by The Compton Press Ltd
The Old Brewery, Tisbury, Wiltshire and
the Dovecote Press, Stanbridge, Wimborne, Dorset

ISBN 0 900193 74 3

Distributed by Michael Russell (Publishing) Ltd
The Chantry House, South Street, Wilton, Wiltshire

Designed by Humphrey Stone
and edited by David Burnett
and printed in England by
BAS Printers Limited, Over Wallop, Hampshire

Contents

Foreword

BY SIR CECIL BEATON

No one could be better qualified than Robert Lassam, Curator of the Fox Talbot Museum, Lacock, to write about William Henry Fox Talbot. In this book he has laid bare the man's genius by explaining his many interests and achievements. We are guided through the truly remarkable evolution of photography and are shown many of the extraordinary photographs he created. Historically of interest because they are amongst the earliest in existence, they include the faces of his friends and neighbours and their families, the landscape of his beloved Wiltshire, and his favourite possessions, some of which are still at Lacock Abbey.

Intelligent, energetic and enthusiastic, blessed with a remarkably fertile mind, it would perhaps seem inevitable that he should make his mark as an innovator. But I believe that few people have ever made so creditable a success as a scholar, a scientist, an inventor, an English landowner, and a Member of Parliament.

Fox Talbot took hold of and made the most of what life offered him: the pleasures of music, literature, poetry and scientific discussion. At the same time he somehow developed the strong quality of aesthetic perception so apparent in his photographs. As he himself once said, 'A casual gleam of sunshine, or a shadow thrown across a path . . . may awaken picturesque imaginings.' Fox Talbot knew instinctively how to compose a picture, and his photographs have a quiet beauty that lifts them above the nature of mere documents; they are bold and simple, redolent of sweet nostalgic charm.

On the pages that follow you will see the fruits of his inspiration, delightfully intimate, poignant, and affectionate portraits of his wife and daughters, stovepipe-hatted men, old ladies, family groups and family picnics, gamekeepers, woodmen, butler and footmen taking tea in a courtyard, books on shelves, Paris roof-tops, a London bridge.

Fox Talbot made a significant contribution, not only to photography, but to the international advancements of knowledge and to the enhancement of enjoyment. It is right that we should be made aware of its full extent in Robert Lassam's delightful book.

Cecil Beaton

Acknowledgements

This book could not possibly have been produced without the generous help of many friends. I am most grateful to Anthony Burnett-Brown, the owner of the Lacock Abbey Collection, and Miss Janet Burnett-Brown, for permission to reproduce Fox Talbot's photographs and for reading the first draft of the text. I also owe a debt of thanks to Mr H.J.P. Arnold, Fox Talbot's biographer, for his advice and guidance. Further thanks are due to The National Trust, Mr Brian Coe, Curator of the Kodak Museum, Mr John Ward of the Science Museum, and to the photograpers Mrs Cristel Amiss and Mr Michael Seaborne, as well as to Mrs Veronica Aplin for typing the drafts of the Introduction. I am also grateful to Sir Cecil Beaton for his kindness in providing the Foreword. My final thanks are to my editor, Mr David Burnett, and to the book's designer, Mr Humphrey Stone, for their continual encouragement during the months I have been working on the book.

ROBERT LASSAM

Introduction

WILLIAM HENRY FOX TALBOT was born in 1800 and died at his family home, Lacock Abbey, Wiltshire, in 1877. In some ways he was a typical English country gentleman. He was a fairly tall, well built man, with receding hair and a preoccupied, almost absent-minded manner. He travelled widely, sat as a Member of Parliament, and managed his estate; but his curiosity and immense intelligence saved him from becoming yet another well-to-do Victorian squire with a taste for science. Fox Talbot's achievements are not in doubt. He invented the polarizing microscope, determined a method for measuring the distance between fixed stars, worked on the design of a linear motor, was one of a handful of scholars capable of translating Assyrian cuneiform, pioneered photo-engraving, was an influential botanist, and perhaps most important of all, he invented the negative/positive process—an invention from which all photography now stems.

Yet Fox Talbot was not only an inventor, but an aesthetic and creative photographer whose work has often been overshadowed by the importance of the negative/positive technique. Many of his photographs have been preserved, and his honest approach to their composition reflects his character and background. He was born and spent part of his childhood at Melbury, a country house in Dorset filled with beautiful paintings and objects. His father, William Davenport Talbot, died when he was only six months old, and his mother, Lady Elisabeth Fox-Strangways, the cultured eldest daughter of the 2nd Earl of Ilchester, had a powerful and lasting influence on his future.

In 1811 Fox Talbot was sent to Harrow, and a year later he wrote and published his first book, *The Flora and Fauna of Harrow*. It was obvious from the start that he was a brilliant child. He quickly mastered Hebrew, French, Italian, Latin and Greek, showed promise as a mathematician, and developed a lifelong fascination for Botany and Chemistry. In 1817 he went up to Trinity College, Cambridge, and in his four years at university won prizes for Mathematics and Greek verse, and was awarded the Chancellor's Medal for 'the best appearance in classical learning.'

Fox Talbot left Cambridge in 1821, the year of his own twenty-first birthday, going first to Paris to stay with his mother and then continuing on through Switzerland and Italy. Intelligent, wealthy, his interests already formed, he had by then decided on a policy that was to shape his entire career. In a letter to his mother he wrote: 'There is nothing like having two or three different pursuits *pour se delasser* when anything goes wrong.' It was a maxim he never forgot. Even when involved in his most crucial photographic discoveries he rarely neglected his other interests. And though it can be argued that they were so wide-ranging and varied that his photographic work suffered, he remains a perfect example of someone who refused to accept the limitations imposed by specialization. In an age when research grants were unknown he mastered not one skill, but many, and managed to add to the knowledge and understanding of each of them. Indeed, the breadth of Fox Talbot's mind makes his invention of the negative/positive process all the more remarkable, and at the same time helps explain the variety of the subject matter in his photographs.

Daguerrotype portrait of Fox Talbot taken by Claudet in 1846.

Six years after leaving Cambridge he took up permanent residence at Lacock Abbey, where as Lord of the Manor he had inherited the village of Lacock and a 1,000 acre estate. In 1832 he became Member of Parliament for Chippenham, holding the seat during the period of the first Reform Parliament and involving himself in the plight of the agricultural labourer at a time when many were rioting in protest at the spread of farm machinery. Ten days after his election he married Constance Mundy, daughter of a Derbyshire landowner, later to bear him three daughters and a son.

But Fox Talbot was not content to spend the rest of his days enjoying the leisurely life of the English country squire, and after his mother and her second husband, a retired naval captain, came to live at Lacock the Abbey became a centre for musical evenings, literary gatherings and scientific discussion. The Irish poet, Thomas Moore, was a frequent visitor to the thirteenth-century nunnery acquired by the Talbots during the Reformation, and the soirées organized by Fox Talbot's mother allowed him to keep in contact with the leading figures in the arts and sciences.

Even before his marriage Fox Talbot had begun to devote much of his time to scientific study, and though he showed concern for the welfare of his tenants and took an interest in various alterations being made to the Abbey (the most significant of which was the completion of the South Gallery with its Oriel Window, later to be the subject of his oldest extant photographic negative), he was already beginning to attract attention as an original and innovative thinker. In 1826 he published *Some Experiments in Coloured Flames,* arguing that substances could be classified by the colours they generated when burnt. Five years later, after reports of these and other experiments reached other scientists, in particular Sir David Brewster and Sir John Herschel, he was elected a Fellow of the Royal Society for his work on mathematics and science.

Fox Talbot's interest in photography, and his approach to the art of taking photographs, can be traced to the October of 1833. He was 'amusing' himself on the shores of Lake Como 'attempting' to make sketches with the aid of the camera lucida (an optical aid to drawing) when the possibility of using chemicals to fix the image first occurred to him. Many years later he wrote:

I then thought of trying again a method which I had tried many years before. This method was to take a camera obscura and to throw the image of the objects on a piece of paper in its focus—fairy pictures, creations of a moment, and destined as rapidly to fade

Lacock Abbey, the West Front.

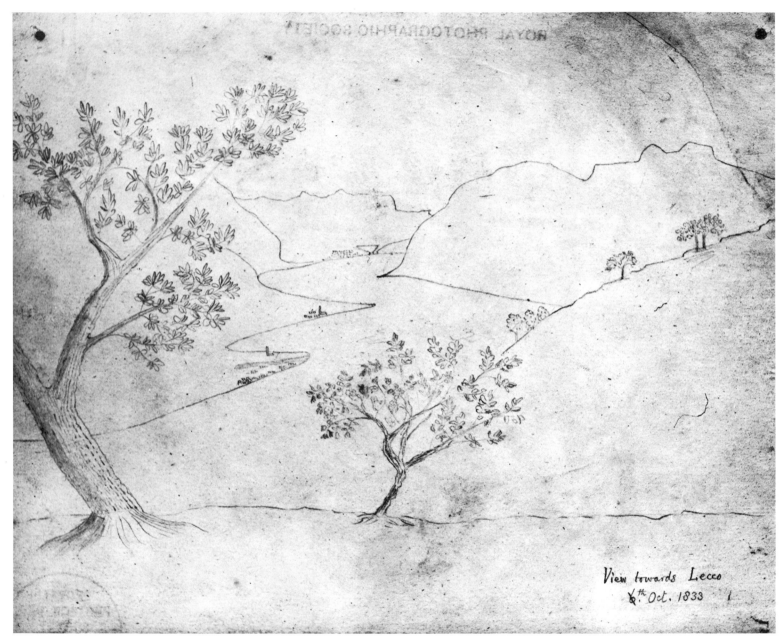

Sketch made by Fox Talbot, with the help of the Camera Obscura, at Lake
Como in October 1833.

away. It was during these thoughts that the idea occurred to me—how charming it would be if it were possible to cause these natural images to imprint themselves durably, and remain fixed upon the paper.

After returning to Lacock he began his experiments. By selecting special paper able to resist disintegration when immersed in chemicals and bathing it in salt solution and silver nitrate he was able to form silver chloride, a light-sensitive salt, insoluble in water, within the paper. The final result was his earliest photogenic drawings – images of leaves and pieces of lace which he pressed against the prepared paper and exposed to sunlight.

He next concentrated on using the paper to record the object seen through the camera obscura. His first cameras were wooden boxes fitted with large diameter lenses, 'little mouse traps' his wife once called them, which he left in position round the Abbey for up to an hour. In 1835 he was able to produce the earliest known photographic negative, that of the Oriel Window. The original negative is barely an inch square and is now preserved in the Science Museum, London.

It is hard for us to understand how Fox Talbot must have felt. Like any inventor working on a new science an immense amount of experiment was needed before the theory became a reality. Yet it is even harder to understand why he then waited four years before announcing his discovery to the public. For it was not until 1839 that he finally submitted a selection of photographs to the Royal Institution. His family was well aware of his achievement, but no word of it became public, and it seems possible that he was hoping to perfect the process before revealing it. We know that he spent part of the period doing research into spectroscopy, passing

The oldest existing negative, the Oriel Window, Lacock Abbey. Fox Talbot photographed the window in August 1835, and beside the negative wrote: 'When first made, the squares of glass about 200 in number could be counted, with help of a lens.'

Replica of the type of camera used by Fox Talbot to take the photograph of the Oriel Window in 1835.

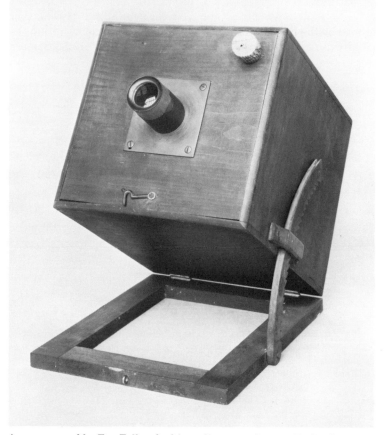

A camera used by Fox Talbot for his earliest experiments. Both telescopic and microscopic lenses could be fitted.

sunlight through glass and then examining the beam through a prism. But whatever the reason for the delay, it is to be regretted, for instead of establishing his claim to be the inventor of photography, his announcement appeared at the same time as that of Daguerre.

It seems extraordinary that as a member of the Royal Society with access to information on scientific research being carried out on both sides of the Channel, Fox Talbot should have known nothing about the pioneering work being done by Niépce and Daguerre in France. But when, in January 1839, *The Gazette de France* reported Daguerre's discovery of a photographic method and the astronomer François Arago lectured on it to the Paris Academy of Sciences, Fox Talbot was genuinely astounded. 'I was placed,' he said later, 'in a very unusual dilemma, for I was threatened with the loss of all my labours.' To establish his own claim as the inventor of photography he sent samples of his work to London. Amongst them were:

flowers and leaves; a pattern of lace; figures taken from painted glass; a view of Venice copied from an engraving; some images formed by the Solar Microscope; various pictures representing the architecture of my house in the country . . . made with the Camera Obscura in the summer of 1835.

A week later, on 31 January, he explained his process to the Royal Society in a paper entitled 'Some Account of the Art of Photogenic Drawing', or 'the process by which natural objects may be made to delineate themselves without the aid of an artist's pencil.'

Once Fox Talbot had revealed his formula for sensitising paper, it was not long before the print sellers, Ackermann of the Strand, were producing outfits to make sensitized paper and selling packets of pre-sensitized paper. Photography for all was now possible.

Fox Talbot's earliest photogenic drawings were all reversed: the lights were dark and the shadows were light, and the picture itself faced the wrong way. In February 1835 he realized that these faults could be corrected. As long as the original could be preserved it could afterwards be copied; 'and by means of this second process the lights and shadows are brought back to their original disposition.' It was left to Sir John Herschel to give them the names they are known by today. The original reversed picture he named the *negative,* its copy he called the *positive.* By discovering the negative/positive process Fox Talbot had revolutionized the future of photography; for by working from a single negative he was able to produce any number of positive prints. It was an astonishing discovery, and like so many pioneering inventions, remarkably simple.

During 1840 Fox Talbot continued to develop his process. By using a mixture of silver nitrate, acetic acid and gallic acid (made from an infusion of nut-gall) he was able to improve the sensitivity of his paper and reduce the exposure time needed for each photograph down to half-a-minute. He also discovered that the sensitized paper kept longer and need not be inserted in the camera immediately after it had been coated. He next realized that it was not essential to

List of subjects photographed by Fox Talbot between 1st March and 18th April 1840. The photograph of the breakfast table, taken on 2nd March, is included amongst the plates.

Three of Fox Talbot's cameras. The sliding box camera on the right
(c. 1845) was bought by Fox Talbot in France.

leave the paper exposed to light in the camera until the image became visible. He had, in short, discovered the 'latent image', for by coating the paper in a solution he named 'gallo-nitrate of silver' both before and after exposure he was able to develop the image after the paper had been taken from the camera.

A year later he decided to patent his discovery. At first he called it the Calotype, from the Greek word for beautiful, *kalos,* but later, after persuasion by friends, he renamed it the Talbotype. Having decided to patent his process he wrote to Herschel telling him of his decision: 'I have taken a patent for the calotype, but nevertheless intend that the use of it shall be entirely free to the scientific world – There appears to be no end to the prospect of scientific research which photography has opened out.' In time Fox Talbot was to forget his original intention to allow unrestricted use of the calotype. Unlike Daguerre, he had received scant recognition and little financial reward for his years of research, and he was later to prosecute some who infringed his patent: a concern for those who had paid a licence fee being uppermost in his mind. But in 1852 he relinquished control of the calotype, except where it was to be used by professional portrait photographers. He did however sell the licence to his process to France and America. The results were not a success. American photographers rebelled at having to pay a licence fee and their sitters preferred to be immortalized by the daguerreotype, for, as Herschel had noted, 'compared to the masterful daguerreotype, Talbot produces nothing but mistiness.' Only later, with the aid of improved lenses, was Talbot able to overcome Herschel's criticism of his early work.

Though Fox Talbot was often frustrated by the commercial aspect of his work, there were some who appreciated and understood the complexity of his research and the stature of his achievement. Brewster, and Herschel, praised him, whilst the French physicist, Jean Baptiste Biot, wrote him a long letter of support, referring both to Daguerre's process and the publicity attending it: 'It is unfortunate for Science to see a man (Daguerre) with such ability always considering the results from the artistic point of view, and never at all from the higher purpose of contributing to the progress of discovery in general.' His half-sister showed an album of his calotypes to Queen Victoria and Prince Albert, 'who admired the great progress made'. His mother was especially delighted with all he had achieved, for she had always known that he had the talent to make an important and original contribution to science. It was she who publicised his work and who pushed him into making prints of the photographs she thought would prove popular; demanding, in one letter, that he 'Pray do some more landscapes or other things from *nature.*'

Whenever he was away from Lacock his wife and assistant continued to make calotypes. As lenses improved, so did the quality of the final print, and Fox Talbot's later photographs of Lacock, life on the estate, London, Paris, as well as his landscape and portrait studies, were to come close to the quality of those of his rival Daguerre. He was a prolific photographer, and in one day in the spring of 1840, when still experimenting, he took photographs of an urn, the garden at

A calotype by Fox Talbot of the South Front of Lacock Abbey,

A painter's eye will often be arrested where ordinary people see nothing remarkable. A casual gleam of sunshine, or a shadow thrown across his path, a time-withered oak, or a moss-covered stone may awaken a train of thoughts and feelings, and picturesque imaginings.

These words remain an accurate reflection of his attitude to the camera and the influence that painting had on his own photography. He was a careful, thoughtful photographer, and the photographs he took at Lacock evoke a vivid portrait of life on an English country estate during the mid-nineteenth century. In some, elegant groups of well-dressed gentry are gathered for tea on the Abbey lawns; in others he shows estate workmen placing a ladder in position, a gamekeeper, or the woodmen. It is this apparent simplicity that makes his work so satisfying. He was a photographer, and he set out to record what he knew best – the English countryside and the way of life it supported. Yet time and again his other interests impose on his choice of subjects – here a leaf, there a fragment of cuneiform; and the complete range of his work does much to explain the character of the man.

Lacock, the south front of the Abbey, an apple branch, a bust of Shakespeare and an antique vase. The difficulties he had to overcome in taking each of them would have defeated many modern photographers. The exposure times were long, the processes complex, and he devoted a great deal of time to composing each photograph before exposing his paper to the image. Many of his photographs are now recognized as masterpieces, and it is worth remembering that while taking them he was simultaneously laying the foundations of the science he had pioneered.

Fox Talbot at home

Fox Talbot once wrote:

We have sufficient authority in the Dutch School of Art for taking as subjects of representation scenes of daily and familiar occurrence.

Fox Talbot's classification of subjects suitable for photogenic drawings, March 1840. On the right he wrote: 'Two or three of these styles might be brought into one drawing and if well combined would make a better specimen of the art.'

At Lacock he found the privacy he needed. For when he walked around a city with his cameras, as he did in York and London in 1845, he was constantly disturbed by crowds of people eager to watch him set up his apparatus – hardly surprising when one remembers that to most of them the camera was a mystery and the making of photographs a form of magic. At Lacock he was near the 'bottle room' where he stored his chemicals and developed his negatives, and was able to continue experimenting with the quality of the final print.

A recent study in the Fox Talbot Museum of the prints made from one negative revealed his concern for their final colour tone. By altering the dilution of his solutions he was able to obtain colours ranging from pale sepia to rich brown. At one time it was thought that these variations were the results of age, but from the outset he was aware of the possibilities of colour toning. In *The Art of Photogenic Drawing* he wrote:

Such is the variety of which the process is capable, that by merely varying the proportions and some trifling details of manipulation, any of the following colours are readily obtainable, sky blue, yellow, rose colour, browns of various shades, black.

Portraiture

Many of the photographs Fox Talbot took at Lacock were portraits, and some, especially those of the estate workers, are early examples of what is now known as photo-journalism. The need to capture what the camera saw was of prime importance to him, and his portraits reveal a sympathetic approach to what remains a difficult branch of photography. The exposure times required a great deal of patience from his sitters, and he himself understood that care and thought were vital to success. He once observed:

When a group of persons has been artistically arrayed, and trained by a little practice to maintain an absolute immobility for a few seconds of time, very delightful pictures are easily obtained. I have observed that family groups are special favourites, and the same five or six individuals may be combined in so many varying attitudes, as to give much interest, and a great air of reality to a series of such pictures.

Reality, again and again he used the word when describing his work.

One advantage of the discovery of the Photographic Art will be, that it will enable us to introduce into our pictures a multitude of minute details which add to the truth and reality of the representation, but which no artist would take the trouble to faithfully copy from nature.

For like most early photographers, Fox Talbot was convinced that photography would record the truth and reality that many contemporary artists were striving to give their work. The camera, he thought, would reveal the blemishes, the imperfections, the details ignored by the painter. And so it did, and by imitating art it freed art from the constraints of naturalism: without photography, it can be argued, there would have been no Impressionism.

Fox Talbot understood his medium, and his own photographic portraits emphasize the freedom of subject matter so fundamental to photography.

Still life

For most of his still life work Fox Talbot used simple domestic items, things he would have come across walking round the Abbey and which appealed to him as suitable for photographs – the china on the breakfast table, books in the library, individual pots, bonnets on a shelf. He left them as he found them, concentrating on placing his camera to take best advantage of the relationship between mass, space and light. *The Open Door,* the calotype of a broom leaning against an open doorway, is a perfect example of his use of light and shadow and of his belief that the photographer could produce a work of art equal to that of the artist.

Composite photograph of the Reading Establishment, founded by Fox Talbot (who may be the man in the centre foreground) in 1843 for the production of prints.

Eleven years after standing on the shores of Lake Como he wrote:

Already sundry amateurs have laid down the pencil and armed themselves with chemicals and with camerae obscurae. These amateurs especially, and they are not a few, who find the rules of perspective difficult to learn and to apply – and who, moreover, have the misfortune to be lazy – prefer to use a method which dispenses with all trouble.

The Reading Establishment

In 1843, after experimenting with the Calotype process for three years, Fox Talbot felt confident that he had mastered his methods and was able to produce photographs whose quality was consistent. He now decided to produce prints for publication and sale.

After some deliberation he selected a former school in Reading as the place to produce photographs in quantity. The school was halfway between Lacock and London, and it seems probable that he chose the site in the hope of being able to supply photographic papers to the studios now opening in London. He appointed a manager, Nicholas Henneman, and converted a greenhouse into the printing works. After a rather hesitant start, production improved, and in seven months 10,400 prints were made from his waxed master negatives at a cost of £237·0·9½d. The waxing was done to improve the translucence of the negative, and some of the prints were sold at Lovejoy's stationery shop in Reading, a well-known literary and scientific local meeting place.

Amongst the photographs made at the Reading Establishment Studio were portraits and copies of paintings, as well as prints from Fox Talbot's own stock of negatives. The list of subjects was later extended by using negatives made by other early users of Fox Talbot's process, amongst them the Reverend Messrs Calvert Jones and Bridges, both of whom had travelled widely through Europe taking photographs of landscapes and buildings.

Invoice listing the stock of calotypes held at the Reading Establishment in 1846.

But the most important production Fox Talbot undertook at Reading was undoubtedly the six issues of *The Pencil of Nature,* the first book to be placed on sale with photographic illustrations. In keeping with the spirit of innovation that had led to his discoveries and inspired the book, he chose a quotation from Virgil for the title page: 'It is a joyous thing to be the first to cross a mountain.' The distinguished American photo-historian, Beaumont Newhall, who once referred to it as the 'Gutenberg Bible of Photography', has described it as a 'show book, an account of the history of the invention, and a demonstration of its accomplishments . . . occasionally offering predictions not realized for decades.'

Fox Talbot chose 24 illustrations for the book and wrote the introducution as well as the text that accompanies each of them. He wrote in a lucid but romantic literary style, outlining his philosophy towards his invention and his aesthetic reasons for his choice of pictures. At times he may seem long-winded and to be stating the obvious; but he was a scientist, photography was still in its infancy, and he regarded *The Pencil of Nature* as a vehicle for setting down on paper the theories he had proved during the years of experiment – both as an inventor and as a photographer. This is how he described Plate V, *The Bust of Patroclus:*

A statue may be placed in any position with regards to the sun . . . the directness of obliquity of the illumination causing of course an immense difference to the effect. And when a choice has been made of the direction in which the sun's rays shall fall, the statue may then be turned round on its pedestal, which produces a second set of variations no less considerable than the first. And when to this is added the change of size which is produced on the image by bringing the Camera Obscura nearer to the statue, or removing it further off, it becomes evident how a very great number of different effects may be obtained from a single specimen of sculpture.

Such meticulousness was typical of Fox Talbot, and the more one looks at his photographs the more one is aware of the thought that went into their composition. Some of his arrangements resulted in photographs that anticipated the work of the best modern photographers, others mirror the tone and character of the age through which he lived.

Frontispiece of the first volume of *The Pencil of Nature,* published in 1844. The Latin inscription, taken from Virgil's *Georgics,* reads: 'It is a joyous thing to be the first to cross a mountain.'

A portrait of Fox Talbot taken by Moffatt of Edinburgh in 1866.

It is unfortunate that he chose not to include any portraits in *The Pencil of Nature,* for the specimens in the Lacock Abbey Collection reveal a charm of composition worthy of the paintings of the period. But it seems that he was determined to avoid stressing the links between the two arts, for in his introductory remarks he wrote:

The little work now presented to the public is the first attempt to publish a series of plates of pictures wholly executed by the new art of Photogenic Drawing, without any aid whatever from the artist's pencil.

The total production of *The Pencil of Nature* ran to 1,016 booklets of the six parts: 286 were printed of the first, 89 of the

The notice to the reader inserted in each copy of *The Pencil of Nature*

sixth. Some of the completed series were specially bound, and a subscription list was raised headed by Queen Victoria; whilst Fox Talbot gave a few to his family and near relatives. Today, very few of the bound volumes still exist, and those that do are immensely valuable. Fox Talbot himself sold the parts for 7/6*d*, 12/-, and 21/-. Some of the prints from *The Pencil of Nature* have been included in this collection of his work.

Fox Talbot produced three other books at the Reading Establishment. The first, *Sun Pictures of Scotland,* was based on the works of Sir Walter Scott. Fox Talbot took the photographs for the book, but they lack the variety of subject matter found in *The Pencil of Nature.* The *Sun Pictures of Scotland* seems to have been a deliberate attempt to repeat the success of his predecessor, but Fox Talbot's third book, *The Talbotype Applied to Hieroglyphics,* though it contained only three illustrations, allowed Fox Talbot to use photography to explain one of his other interests. The final publication, now extremely rare, was the *Annals of the Artists of Spain* by William Stirling, the Scottish historian. The book included 66 copies of paintings, engravings and drawings chosen by Stirling, who himself acknowledged his debt to Fox Talbot by saying in the preface; 'The following illustrations my friends are indebted to the beautiful photographic process invented by Mr Fox Talbot.'

Though the publication of *The Pencil of Nature* was to mark the summit of Fox Talbot's own career as a photographer, he continued to try and improve the quality of the calotype. He experimented with glass as a support for sensitised solution and lodged two patents for his work. But in 1851 Frederick Scott Archer invented the collodion process, and within five years both the calotype and daguerretype had been made redundant. The Reading

Calotype by Fox Talbot of an Egyptian tablet.

Establishment was closed in 1847 and after the eventual failure and closure of a London shop run by his manager, Hennemann, much of the stock was returned to Lacock Abbey. It now forms the basis of the three major collections of his work in Britain; those at the Fox Talbot Museum, the Science Museum, and the Royal Photographic Society.

When one of his photographic patents expired in 1855, Fox Talbot did not renew it, and he turned his attentions to photo-engraving, mathematics, motive power and Assyrian cuneiform translation. In the summer of 1877 he was asked to write an appendix to Tissandier's *History and Handbook of Photography*. On 12 September he wrote: 'I have not been well, which has delayed my sending you the rest of my paper. I am now sending you the second part, the third part is in preparation and will complete the appendix.' The work was never to be completed. His health became worse, and he died in his study at Lacock in the early hours of Monday, 17 September 1877.

Many obituaries followed his death, but perhaps the most accurate assessment of his achievement was contained in a book first published in 1853. In its preface the author wrote:

The discovery of the art of photography is due to Mr Fox Talbot, who, early in 1839, communicated to the world the result of his experiments and an account of the process by which they were conducted. The discovery was so startling and its capabilities so wonderful, that the whole scientific world was interested in them, and directed its attention to their development; with what result we need not inquire, for the evidence abounds on every side.

The evidence continues to abound, for the camera has become part of our way of life. Yet the plates in this present book are not just a memorial to Fox Talbot's genius as an inventor. His photographic inventions had one purpose, to allow him to creatively interpret and reveal some truth about the world around him. The photographs in this book are proof of his success.

Chronology of Fox Talbot's Life

1800 Born on 11 February at Melbury, Dorset, the home of the Earl of Ilchester.
His father, Davenport Talbot, dies on July 31st.
William Henry Fox Talbot's earliest years were spent at Melbury, Bowood in Wiltshire and Penrice Castle in South Wales.

1804 His mother marries Captain Feilding RN.

1808 Sent to the Reverend Thomas R. Hooker's Preparatory School, Rottingdean, Sussex.

1811 Entered Harrow School.
Published with W. C. Trevelyan *The Flora and Fauna of Harrow*.

1815 Left Harrow for further tutorial study in Castleford, Yorkshire.

1817–1821 Entered Trinity College, Cambridge.
Became 12th Wrangler (in Mathematics) 1821, obtained the Porson Prize for Greek verse 1820, awarded Chancellor's Classical Medal 1821.

1821 Inherited Lacock Abbey estates.

1827 Resident at Lacock Abbey as Lord of the Manor.

1831 Elected Fellow of the Royal Society.

1831 Elected as Whig Member of Parliament for Chippenham.
Marries Constance Mundy of Markeaton, Derbyshire.

1835 Birth of first daughter, Ela.
After experiments with salted paper and silver nitrate in 1834 produces the first negative of the Oriel Window, Lacock Abbey.

1837 Birth of second daughter, Rosamond.

1838 Royal Medal for researches in integral calculus

1839 Birth of third daughter, Matilda.

1840 Early calotype pictures recorded.

1841 Patent taken out for his calotype process.
Patent in coating and colouring of metallic surfaces.

1842 Patent for gilding and silvering medals.
Birth of a son, Charles Henry.
Paper on production of reflecting telescopes to the British Association.
Royal Society presents Fox Talbot with the Rumford Medal.

1843 Begins production at the Reading Establishment of prints for sale.

1844 Issues first of the six volumes of *The Pencil of Nature*.

1845 Experiments with heat engines.

1850 Largely devoted to Assyrian cuneiform translation.

1852 Motive power patent for linear electric motor.
Further improvements in the art of engraving.

1854 Published notes on the Assyrian inscriptions
Translates clay cylinder of the Assyrian, King Tiglath Pileser.

1855 Awarded Grande Medaille d'Honneur at the Exposition Universale, Paris.

1858 Photographic Society of Scotland awards Fox Talbot its gold medal for discovery of photography.
Second patent in photo-engraving.

1863 Elected honorary member of the Photographic Society.

1877 Dies at Lacock Abbey on Monday 17 September.

Published Works by Fox Talbot

W.H.F. Talbot & W.C. Trevelyan, *The Flora and Fauna of Harrow* (London 1812)

Legendary Tales in Verse and Prose (James Ridgeway, London 1830).

Hermes: or Classical and Antiquarian Researches, No. 1 (Longman, Orme, Brown, Green & Longmans, London 1838)

Hermes, No. 2 (1839)

The Antiquity of the Book of Genesis: illustrated by Some New Arguments (Longman, Orme, Brown, Green & Longmans, London 1839)

The Pencil of Nature (Longman, Orme, Brown, Green & Longmans, London, issued in six parts between June 1844 and April 1846).

Sun Pictures in Scotland (published by subscription, 1845)

English Etymologies (John Murray, London 1847)

The Talbotype Applied to Hieroglyphic (Longman, Orme, Brown, Green & Longmans, London 1854)

G. Tissandier, *A History and Handbook of Photography,* containing an Appendix by W.H.F. Talbot completed by his son C.H. Talbot (Sampson Low, Marston, Searle & Rivington, London 1878)

In addition Fox Talbot published a large number of papers in various scientific journals. Of these, the most important to his work as a photographer are:

'An account of the processes employed in photogenic drawing' (Royal Society Proceedings, IV, 1839)

'Some account of the art of photogenic drawing, or the process by which natural objects may be made to delineate themselves without the aid of the artist's pencil' (Royal Society Proceedings, LV, 1839)

'Remarks on M. Daguerre's photogenic process' (British Association Report, Part II, 1839)

'An account of some recent improvements in photography' (Royal Society Proceedings, IV, 1841)

'Photoglyphic engraving' (Photographic News, 22 October 1858)

THE PLATES

Fox Talbot's mother, Lady Elisabeth Fox Strangways. (*c.* 1845, Lacock Abbey Collection)

Fox Talbot's wife, Constance, and their three daughters, a portrait taken in the gardens at Lacock Abbey.
(1842, Science Museum Collection)

Sharington's Tower, Lacock Abbey. (*c.* 1844, Lacock Abbey Collection)

The lake, Lacock Abbey. (Date unknown, Lacock Abbey Collection)

Photogenic drawing of a leaf. (1835, Lacock Abbey Collection)

'A Fruit Piece', Plate XXIV from *The Pencil of Nature*. In order to explain how prints taken
from the same paper negative vary in quality, Fox Talbot wrote alongside the plate:
'the circumstances of light and shade and time of day etc, not corresponding to what they were on a former occasion,
a slightly different but not worse result attended the experiment.' (*c.* 1844, Lacock Abbey Collection)

'The Fruit Sellers', a group portrait taken in the Cloister courtyard, Lacock Abbey.
(1842, Lacock Abbey Collection)

Man in woodyard. (Date unknown, Lacock Abbey Collection)

'The Haystack', calotype chosen for *The Pencil of Nature*. (*c*. 1843, Lacock Abbey Collection)

Seated figure in the Cloisters, Lacock Abbey. Two calotypes printed from the original paper negatives showing the tonal range achieved by Fox Talbot. (Date unknown, Lacock Abbey Collection)

Ancient Vestry, Lacock Abbey.

(see opposite page for caption)

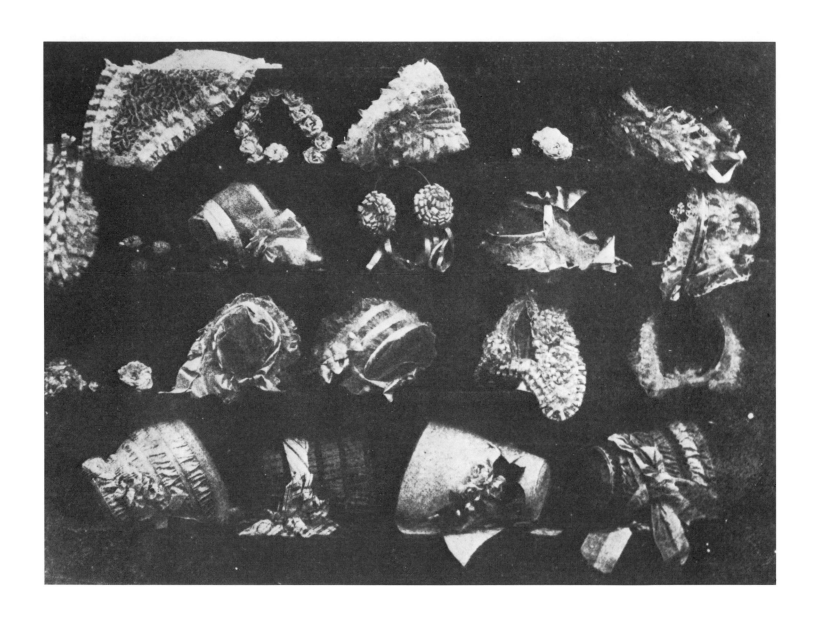

Bonnets in a milliner's shop window. (1846, Lacock Abbey Collection)

Group of ladies at Lacock. (Date unknown, Science Museum Collection)

Two gentlemen shaking hands. (Original calotype retouched with water-colour paints, 1842, Lacock Abbey Collection)

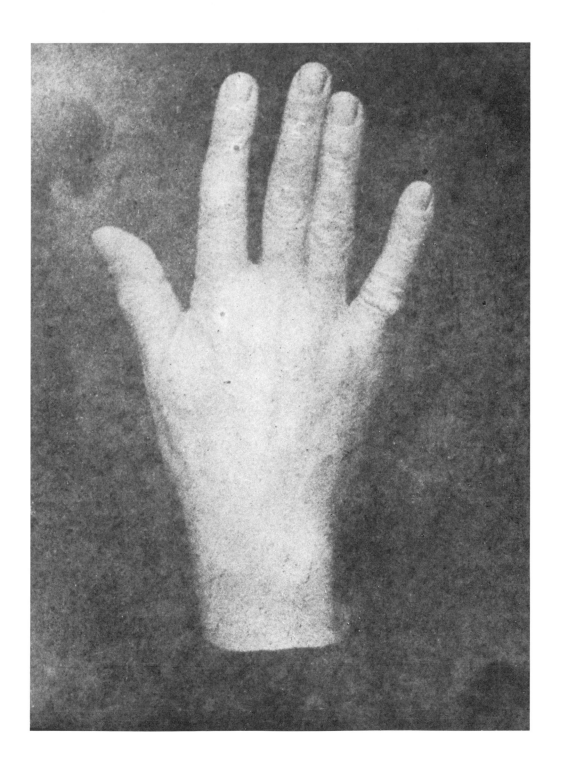

Study of a man's hand. (1840, Science Museum Collection)

The gamekeeper, Lacock Abbey. (Date unknown, Lacock Abbey Collection)

The bricklayers. (Date unknown, Lacock Abbey Collection)

Oak tree in Carclew Park, Cornwall, the home of Sir Charles Lemon, brother-in-law of Lady Elisabeth
Fox Strangways, Fox Talbot's mother. (Date unknown, Lacock Abbey Collection)

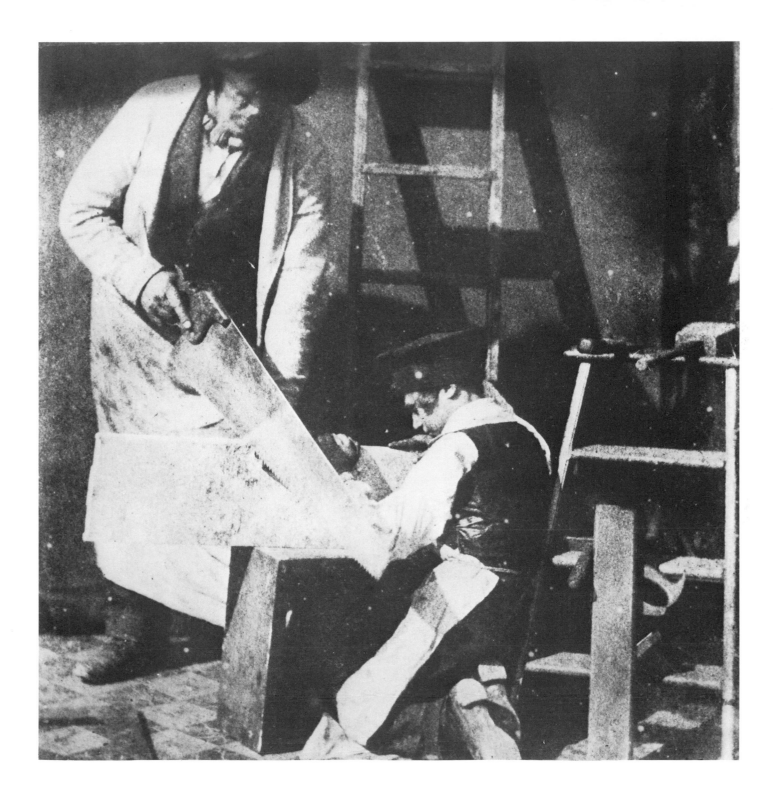

The carpenters. (Date unknown, Lacock Abbey Collection)

Portrait of a lady. (Date unknown, Lacock Abbey Collection)

Portrait of man. (Date unknown, Lacock Abbey Collection)

Portrait of man with books. (Date unknown, Lacock Abbey Collection)

Two shelves of books, Lacock Abbey. (*c.* 1844, Lacock Abbey Collection)

'The Open Door', Plate VI of *The Pencil of Nature*. Alongside the plate Fox Talbot wrote:
'The chief object of the present work is to place on record some of the early beginnings of a new art,
before the period, which we trust is approaching, of its being brought to maturity by
the aid of British talent. (*c*. 1844, Lacock Abbey Collection)

The breakfast table, Lacock Abbey. (1840, Lacock Abbey Collection)

Negative and positive of a photogenic drawing of a leaf. (1845, Lacock Abbey Collection)

Photographic copy of a page in an illustrated book on botany. (Date unknown, Lacock Abbey Collection)

An engraving of Christ's head superimposed on an oak leaf. (1839, Royal Photographic Society Collection)

Portrait of a young lady. (Date unknown, Lacock Abbey Collection)

Photogenic drawing of lace. (Date unknown, Lacock Abbey Collection)

Photogenic drawing of plant. (From one of Fox Talbot's own albums, dated 1835–1839, Lacock Abbey Collection)

Copy of a lithographic print, a Parisian caricature chosen by Fox Talbot for Plate XI of *The Pencil of Nature*.
He states 'that all kinds of engravings may be copied by photographic means; not only as producing in general
nearly fac-simile copies, but because it enables us at pleasure to alter the scale, and to make the copies as much
larger or smaller than the originals as we may desire.' (1844 Lacock Abbey Collection)

Canterbury Cathedral taken from the north-west. (Paper negative, date unknown, Lacock Abbey Collection)

Lovejoy's Library, Reading, with a display of mounted calotypes in the window. The shop was used as a sales outlet by the Reading Establishment. (*c.* 1845, Lacock Abbey Collection)

Antoine Claudet. (Date unknown, Lacock Abbey Collection)

Interior of Claudet's studio; Claudet is in the centre.
(Date unknown, Science Museum Collection)

Interior of Claudet's studio. This photograph was taken shortly after that on the page opposite.
(Date unknown, Science Museum Collection)

Corner of the Rue de la Paix and the Rue Casanova, Paris. (1843, Lacock Abbey Collection)

Orleans Cathedral, detail of tracery. (1843, Lacock Abbey Collection)

The Bridge of Orleans, taken from the south bank of the Loire and chosen by Fox Talbot as
Plate XII of *The Pencil of Nature.* (*c.* 1843, Lacock Abbey Collection)

Two views of *Eve at the Fountain,* a maquette by E.H. Bailey (April 1840, Lacock Abbey Collection)

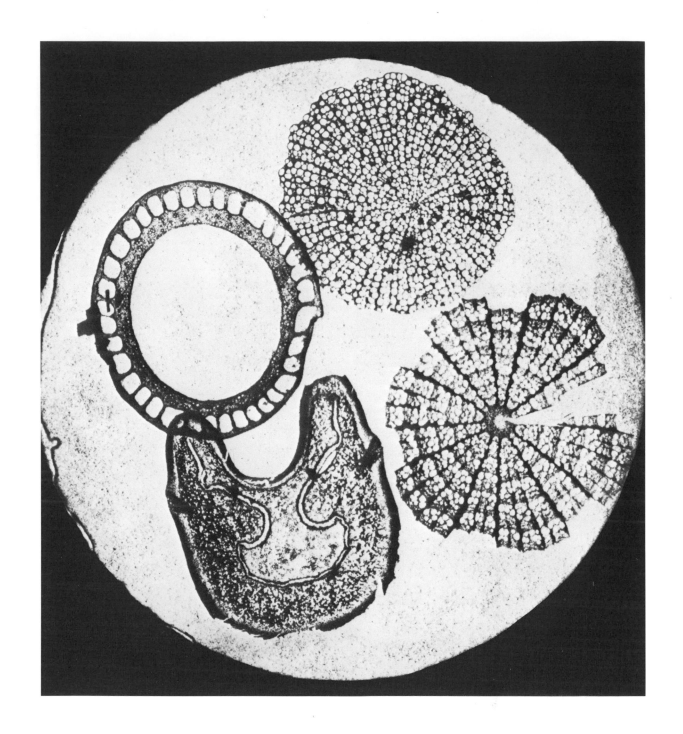

Photomicrograph of a plant stem section. (1839, Lacock Abbey Collection)

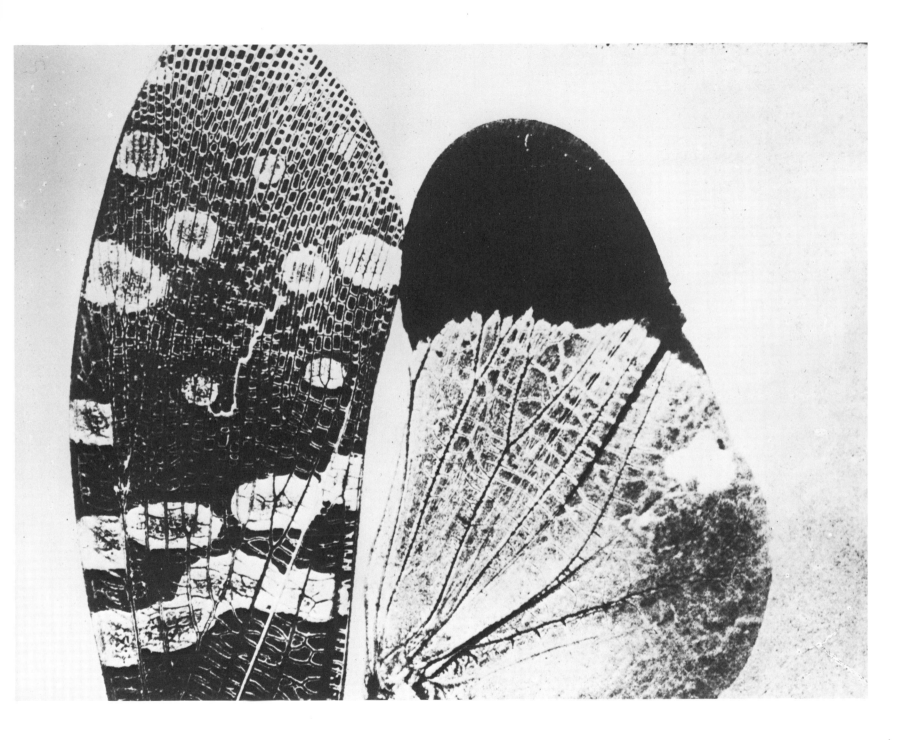

Photomicrograph of the wing of a Lantern fly. (1839, Lacock Abbey Collection)

Photogenic drawing of a leaf. (*c.* 1836, Science Museum Collection)

Still life of small sculpted figure. (April 1840, Lacock Abbey Collection)

Three men. (Date unknown, Lacock Abbey Collection)

The High Street, Oxford. (Date unknown, Lacock Abbey Collection)

Portrait of woman and child. (Date unknown, Lacock Abbey Collection)

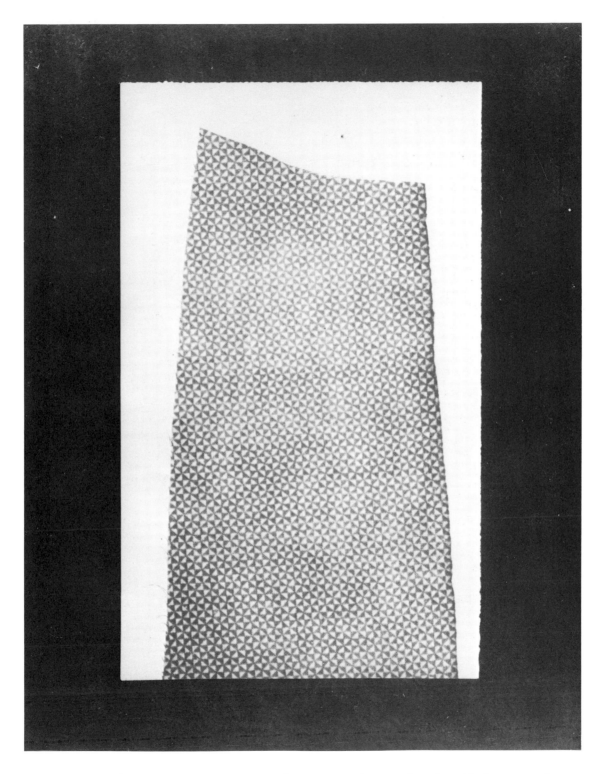

Gauze pattern. Fox Talbot later used gauze to produce a screen when experimenting with photo-engraving.
(Date unknown, Lacock Abbey Collection)

Place de la Carousel, Paris. (1843, Science Museum Collection)

The base of Nelson's Column, Trafalgar Square, before the addition of Landseer's lions.
(1845, Lacock Abbey Collection)

Ruins of country house. (Date unknown, Lacock Abbey Collection)

The Royal Pavilion, Brighton. (1846, Science Museum Collection)

The approach to York from the river. (1845, Science Museum Collection)

Hungerford Suspension Bridge, taken from the north bank of the Thames.
(1845, Lacock Abbey Collection)

The Madeleine Church, Paris. (1843, Lacock Abbey Collection)

Malines Cathedral, Belgium, seen over the city rooftops. (1846, Lacock Abbey Collection)

'The Ladder', taken in the stable-yard at Lacock Abbey, Plate XIV in *The Pencil of Nature*.
(1844, Lacock Abbey Collection)

Two figures at Lacock Abbey. (Date unknown, Lacock Abbey Collection)

Negative and positive of the Chess Players. The French photographer Claudet, in whose studio
the photograph was taken, is sitting on the right. (Date unknown, Lacock Abbey Collection)

Tree in winter. (Date unknown, Lacock Abbey Collection)

Elm tree at Lacock. (Date unknown, Lacock Abbey Collection)

The woodyard, Lacock Abbey. (Date unknown, Lacock Abbey Collection)

A rare early snow photograph, taken by Fox Talbot in the grounds of Lacock Abbey.
(Date unknown, Lacock Abbey Collection)

Fox Talbot's daughters. (*c.* 1842, Lacock Abbey Collection)

NOTE ON ILLUSTRATIONS

The illustrations in this book were copied on special film from Fox Talbot's original photographs. No retouching has been carried out in the reproduction of these, and any brush marks and spots shown are on the original calotypes.